OPEN
DOORS
PUBLISHING

We Hear You

American Kids' Reflections on Darfur

"My responsibility to humanity is to be a voice for others."

-Neha Agrawal

We Hear You

American Kids' Reflections on Darfur

Authors and Illustrators
Mill Run Elementary School Poets for Peace

Editors
Students at Thomas Jefferson School of
Science and Technology

Collaborating Teachers
Logan Stacy Williams
Rebecca Nellum Williams
Ann Rovang-Wolff

Art Teacher
Lynn Portch

Cover Photo
Courtesy of Darfur Diaries
www.darfurdiaries.org

Cover Design
Arthur Myhre Scott

Authors' proceeds from the sale of this book support the Darfur School Project. The Darfur Peace and Development Organization started the Darfur School Project to support schools in Darfur. The project's goal is to pay teacher salaries and purchase supplies for students so their academic achievement can be sustained. www.dpado.org

We Hear You:
American Kids' Reflections on Darfur

Published by Open Doors Publishing, LLC
11654 Plaza American Drive #267
Reston, VA 20190

Copyright © 2007 by Logan Williams

Foreword © 2007 by Dr. Maya Angelou
"A Pledge to Rescue Our Youth" © 2006 by Maya Angelou
Reprinted by permission of the author

Introduction © 2007 by Aisha Bain, Jen Marlowe, and Adam Shapiro

Cover Photo courtesy of *Darfur Diaries:Stories of Survival*

Printed in the United States of America
Library of Congress Cataloging-in-Publication Data

ISBN- 10: 0-9796750-0-6
ISBN 13: 978-0-9796750-0-3

Book design by Soren Bakken and Logan Williams

For the children in Darfur—
our friends

Foreword

The courageous person knows that all children are our children as we belong to the world and the world belongs to us. *We Hear You American Kids' Reflections on Darfur* project, along with their teachers' guidance, care about Ireland and Bosnia, and South Africa, and China, and Darfur..., and Darfur. Thank you, Mrs. Rebecca Nellum Williams, Ms. Logan Williams, Mrs. Ann Rovang-Wolff, and Mill Run students for your courage.

Joy,
Maya Angelou

A Pledge to Rescue Our Youth
written by Maya Angelou © 2006

Young women, young men of color, we add our voices to the voices of your ancestors who speak to you over ancient seas and across impossible mountain tops.

> Come up from the gloom of national neglect, you have already been paid for.

> Come out of the shadow of irrational prejudice, you owe no racial debt to history.

> The blood of our bodies and the prayers of our souls have bought you a future free from shame and bright beyond the telling of it.

We pledge ourselves and our resources to seek for you clean and well-furnished schools, safe and non-threatening streets, employment which makes use of your talents, but does not degrade your dignity.

> You are the best we have.
> You are all we have.
> You are what we have become.

We pledge you our whole hearts from this day forward.

Introduction

A few months ago, we received an email from a fifth-grade teacher in Virginia named Logan Williams. She had encountered our book "Darfur Diaries" and had decided to educate her fifth grade students about the atrocities taking place in Darfur, connecting them to previous horrors, such as what the class had been reading about in Lois Lowry's "Number the Stars". She sent us a packet of poetry that the fifth graders at her school, Mill Run Elementary, had written in response to learning about and talking about Darfur.

We read page after page of the fifth graders' writing, amazed at the compassion, empathy, outrage and solidarity for the children of Darfur that was expressed so powerfully in each poem.

These young authors realized that knowing was not enough. They understood that it is their actions, including speaking out, that is most important. When we went to eastern Chad and Darfur in the fall of 2004, we had a very simple goal; to bring back the stories that no one was telling at that time; or rather, that no one was willing to tell. It was almost as if we were responding to the provocative question Elizabeth Kellen posed in her poem several years later, directed at each and every one of us:

> *Why do we watch,*
> *just standing around*
> *doing nothing?*

Students have been among the people doing the most on this issue. Students at Harvard got the university to stop investing in an oil company that was doing business with the government of Sudan-a tactic called "divestment" that was part of how the international community helped end apartheid in South Africa. Students at Oak Park River

High School near Chicago raised $6,000 for us to start funding a school for the kids we met in Muzbat village in Darfur. Sixth grade students in Minneapolis made a CD that they sold all over their community and used the proceeds to help people in Darfur. Students can-and really have-taken the lead. However, among all the incredible examples of student activism, the young activists at Mill Run are extraordinary, not only because of their youth-but because of the clarity with which they understand that the fear and trauma of a child from Darfur is as demanding of the world's attention as their own fear and trauma would be. This is a clarity that most of us in the world needs more of.

May this book serve as an inspiration to anyone who encounters it, young or old, to become more fully engaged in our world. We hope the poetry within these pages will provoke all of us to examine what is worth caring about and what is worth acting on.

We were speaking once about Darfur to a 9th grade class in Seattle, WA. One boy raised his hand and said, "Why should I care about something that is happening across the world from me, in Sudan, when there are problems in my backyard, in my own neighborhood? Shouldn't I get involved in those issues?"

Our response to him was, "If this film and this discussion motivates you to get involved in your own community, in something happening in the world around you, no matter how close or far, then that's fantastic."

To the readers of this book: Our greatest hope is that "We Hear You" will inspire you to get engaged in the world-whether it's in what's happening in Darfur, in Haiti, Iraq, Afghanistan or in your community. We are all responsible.

To parents and teachers: we all share a desire to protect our children from the darker sides of the world. Logan

Williams and her fellow language arts teachers at Mill Run understood, however, that we do not protect our children when we shield them from unjust realities; we protect them when we work in partnership with them to challenge and change those realities. She is an exceptional example of an educator in the truest sense of the word.

To the young poets who wrote "We Hear You": you have set an example for all of us to follow. To discover places in the world where injustice is occurring on a daily basis, to then question, investigate, learn more-and, ultimately, to ask ourselves what we can do and to raise our voices in protest and solidarity-be it in the form of a rally, a documentary film or thought-provoking, searing, compassionate poetry. We applaud you for refusing to quietly tolerate the atrocities you became witness to. You are courageous individuals. But we don't have to tell you that. As Andrew Hoyler wrote in his poem,

> *"Bravery can be unpredictable.*
> *It can happen anywhere."*

We are proud to join forces with Mill Run's brave fifth grade classes in stating loudly and clearly: We will not be silent!

In solidarity,
Aisha Bain, Jen Marlowe, Adam Shapiro
Filmmakers/Authors "Darfur Diaries"

Teachers' Notes

This project started with a historical fiction novel about the Holocaust, *Number The Stars* by Lois Lowry. The students went on the journey with the protagonist, Annemarie, a ten year old who was living in Denmark in 1943. At this time in history, German forces occupied Denmark.

Annemarie is best friends with Ellen, who is Jewish. At the start of the novel, Annemarie believes she is not courageous and is glad that she is an ordinary person who will never be called upon to be brave. Annemarie becomes the heroine in the story and learns that being afraid does not denote a lack of bravery. Doing the right thing, even when one is afraid, constitutes courage.

Next, the class had discussions about friendships, ethics, courage, and bravery. Students were asked to define and identify the inhumane behavior in the novel and in the world today.

We then turned our focus toward present day Darfur. Keeping in mind our readings and discussions, the students were asked the following questions: What is our responsibility to humanity? Can the power of words change history? This prompted the students to reflect on the actions of Dr. Martin Luther King, Jr. during the Civil Rights Movement in the United States. We also studied the powerful words and actions of Dr. Maya Angelou and other courageous individuals.

Our hope was that through the process of answering these questions, both in class discussion and in the poetry they wrote, the students would deepen their belief in their own ability to take a stand. This project gave the students a way to feel more connected and aware, not only of struggles in their own community but also of struggles in the lives of people outside of the United States.

The poetry in this book is a culmination of a journey, beginning with Annemarie and ending in present day Darfur. While writing the poetry, the 5th graders momentarily became the voices of those who are not being heard. Some of the students' words are that of hope, courage, and bravery. Other students lend their voices to the reality of war and life in a refugee camp. They want to let the people of Darfur know that they are not forgotten and that they hear them.

The students are learning that the power of words can change history.

--Logan Stacy Williams, Rebecca <u>Nellum</u> Williams, and Ann Rovang-Wolff

A Dead Dream
Erin Fincher

The dream flies into the air…
nobody saves it.
It lies there,
helplessly,
like a sunken ship in the sea.
It goes to the abyss.
The place where all,
dead dreams go.

A Different World
Tina Ju

There is a place
on Earth
that might seem like
a different world.
Where peace is shattered by cruel
violence.
Where people don't get a chance to unite.

The people there use
force to frighten away
other people from their homes.
A different world.

In every family,
death.
A different world.

Who will protect the world?
We are hopeful and we pray
that there will be peace on Earth.

A Friend
Nic Tercero

I hear the thunder of your cries,
in the simple night.
I may not know you,
but I am a friend.
The wind will send you a message,
whispers of love and hope.

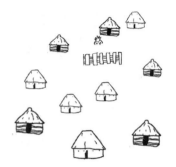

A Haunting
Virginia Ojeda

People say this village is haunted.
There's a smell of death.
Children cry at night.
A haunting.
All anyone can hope for
is that they'll rest in peace some day.

A Journey To Hope
Belle Brewer

How quickly blood is shed,
In this journey to freedom.
How quickly the flesh is torn,
On this path to success.
This world is a world of life,
A world of hope,
And a world of dreams.
Our dream is peace,
Even through this war.
But love,
Love for each other.
Love will stop the war.

A Life Of Sadness
Elizabeth Kellen

Some call it a humanitarian crisis.
Some call it sad.
But through the eyes of a child whose voice means nothing,
this is called life.
Imagine the impact of this poisoned life.
A dark, cramped, cold tent.
Not much food or clean water.
Why do we watch, just standing around
doing nothing?
Every child and every family has a vision
that someday heroes will come and save their world.
That someday, their spirits will find peace.

A New Journey
Austin Winegar

Patience in the dark
Night
All paths lead into
the shadows
A new journey starts tomorrow
Where love is energy
so powerful
The spirits of a thousand
angels' truths
Can make a hero

A Path to Life
Sarah Murphy

Your world may be rocky
Soon, you will dig deep
and find the path to life.
It may seem difficult
but you need to be brave.
The world's love is strong and
will help you hold the shovel.
Soon you will dig deep and
find the path to life.

A Perfect World
Anika Steenstra

I am wishing for a perfect world.
A world where hope is in every corner of the earth
and peace is in every country.
A world where people can see beyond
their differences and love each other.
This is my perfect world.

A Place Where Danger Laughs
Christina Elizabeth Hunter

A child living in Darfur,
Walking along a dark path.
Unseen, sneaking in the shadows.
The feeling of death in the air.
Suddenly becoming scared.
Her body stiffens
She is running and running,
running to find safety.
Hoping it will be help out there –somewhere.
But only finding,
A place where danger laughs.

A Word
Samantha Panizo

Loss has filled the world.
Freedom is only a word.
The air is stale.
It is hard to inhale.
My breath is gone.

All Alone
Alvaro Inmon

I walk the lonely road
Like an island with no land,
Only water
Uneasiness
I feel I am sinking
Only silence
Nothing but silence
I walk alone
My shadow is the only one beside me
Alone on the road of broken dreams
Broken dreams
Alone

All I Want Is Freedom
Rebecca Enzinna

Stillness and silence
All I have left is hope
I cry for help
But the answer is stillness and
silence.
I dream of freedom
Freedom

An Ocean
Daney Carlin

I am swimming
in a bloody ocean.
I am looking
at my friend trapped
in a fishing net.
The fisherman…
they do not care..
I am petrified without her,
Can I still live?
I am swimming
in a bloody ocean.

Angels
Leah Choi

The angels gather around this world
They watch the darkness take over
Its shadows cover the sky
The angels bring light that carries hope
The darkness disappears
As the light surrounds the world

Balance
McKaley Badgett

Life is like a balance beam.
You try so hard to stay on,
you try so hard to get to the end
without falling.
You try.
Imagine you are walking on a beam
in a world where you never fall off.
A world free of fear.

Be Brave
Cal Veatch

Be brave
Trust my words of love
There is hope
Life is in the palm of your hand
You see what you are living for
The spirit of clear hope is rising
Energy builds up and the violence is shattering
The stillness of the shadows slows your anger
Patience builds up inside your body
Because you are no longer discouraged
Because you see your life
in the palm of your hand

Believe
Rachel Morse

We are trying to help, believe
You will be free, believe
If you get sad or worried, have faith
Believe in one world

Blank Paper
Ilana Doroteo

The paint has dried out
The pencils have broken
The clay has hardened
The pastels have
disappeared
There is nothing
but a blank piece of paper

Blown Away
Lauren Goffi

I stand on the sand
My hope is taken by the wind
My dreams are being blown away.
The waves get bigger
and it is harder to see
My dreams are being blown away.

Brave
Jessica Fiermen

I stand there
watching
the people with their
silent screams.
It makes my heart
feel empty inside.
The shadows I see
of all the soldiers
look like spirits
on a journey into the night.
Tears stream down my face
for what I see is wrong.
I do hope that tomorrow
will bring peace once again.

Bravery
Andrew Hoyler

Bravery can be unpredictable.
It can happen anywhere.
Some acts are small and some are large.

The most powerful moments are not always seen.
Bravery is one of the most amazing things in the world.
Kindness and friendship are very powerful.
Everyone can be brave.

Bright Shadow
Maaz Malik

Life is a darkening shadow
Creeping on you,
You turn your back
You try to get away from it
But it runs after you.
You cannot stop it.
But together we can make it bright
And you will come to see,
Your life is one of the brightest lives
There has ever been.

Broken Wings

Reema Malhotra

My life is that of a forgotten bird
My feathers have fallen
I'm paralyzed.
I lay in my nest
with broken wings.

Courage

Kyle McKinny

Having great courage means
being fearless.
We never want anyone we love to die—or worse,
to live in fear of everything.
We want to be as brave as a mountain lion,
but our fear gets in the way.
We must find the courage
and live.

Crying Children
Adam Lewis

I see children crying
with tear-filled eyes.
As they dream that
one day
they might be free.
Heroes,
looking for heroes
to be a guide
for the journey
back home.

Daddy
Sophia Rizzo

Running barefoot,
I let my anger go wild.
Weaving through those left behind.
Don't let the younger kids see your tears.
As you pass your father,
one of the unlucky ones.

Darfur Child
Tristan Miller

I am full of fear and
My vision is blurry
I see a skinny shadow
I hope for peace
I feel close to death
I hear children crying
Like rain on a bad day
I am a child of Darfur

Dark Times
Magid Abdo

The dark side is taking over the city.
Blood shed is everywhere.
We are completely lost.
We have hope that
the light is moving toward us.
Freedom and peace, at last.

Dark Tunnel
Matthew Whitmore

In the dark tunnel of despair,
never give up hope.
No matter how dark the tunnel may be,
the blazing light of freedom
is always at the end.

Deafening
Evan Ricapito

It's cold and wet
Not a sound is heard
It is deafening in the camp
No voice is noticed
"A voice"
holds power
The strength to change
Transform lives
Create dreams
Construct hope
"A voice"
is needed

Death is a Dream?
McKensey Ziegler

Death is the dream
that you hope did not just happen.
The tears that fall from heaven
quiet the earth.
The sadness that is felt
that cannot be explained.
The violence leads to puzzled looks
on the children's faces.
They wonder if death is just a dream.

Distance
Amani Yates

If I knew the distance
I may be frightened.
I can't see.
I need the energy,
the vision, the trust.
If I only knew
the direction to the path.
The path to my spirit.

Do Not
Matthew Wolcott

Do not think without hope
The world is filled with hope
Do not think of life without peace
The world is filled with peace
Do not think of a place without freedom
Think of a life filled with freedom
Do not think of your life without encouragement
I can be your encouragement
Do not think without hope

Dream of Suffering
Q Kersey

I dreamed
that I was a star.
I showed my courage
and faced my fear.
I suffered
so that the kids
would suffer no more.

Edge of Freedom
Brandon Tan

Standing at the edge of freedom...
Thinking of my loss
It has made me cry so much
Rain falls like my tears
Anger burns inside me.
How I wish to be free...

Empty
Jamie Woodall

Everything around me,
empty as can be.
No words are spoken,
I'm running, no sound.
The only thing I hear
is rustling in the bushes,
and boom!
I'm sitting on the ground,
empty as can be.
Nothing around me.

Empty Life
Zach Fossett

Life
should be peaceful and full of hope.
But, not anymore.
Now there are death, tears,
and fear.
Hear this voice.
Imagine what it is like,
to cry in front of your
son's grave.

Fateful Journey
Tommy Roche

The path may seem clouded by darkness,
Clouded by shadows.
But you must have persistence,
You must be heroic.
For one day,
Your lengthy journey into freedom,
Will reach its fate.

Fear in Your Spirit
Eddie Loynab

You have fear in your spirit
and terror in your eyes.
But love will guide you
to the right path.
A peaceful life.
Keep running and running
away from the fear.
Don't let it consume you.
If you have trust and faith
you will make it.
I promise.

Fearless
Nick Jones

The hero stands up,
ready to be brave.
He is fearless as he runs for hope.
The world is watching,
they are ready and waiting for him.

Feel Their Fear
Blake Ratliff

I can feel their fear
It is like a bull charging at me
I can see the look on the
children's faces
It is like a thunderstorm
The children and parents are
in Gods' hands
They are waiting

Free Souls
Sabreena Abedin

On harsh cold nights
I'd dream of a free world
With fairness towards all souls
And hearts full of hope

Freedom From the War
Marcus Givner

Freedom is something that I don't have.
It's been taken away from me.
I must be brave, for I will face a lot of hardships.
Like rain, tears will be falling from the heavens
and birds will be my angels.
I must see the truth
in the war that I'm going through.
If not, the war will consume me.
In the hardships that I face,
I need a friend beside me.
In hopes of the war being over
my spirit will fly free into the heavens of the earth.
Until that day I will be trapped
in my own fear.

Freedom Run
Logan Reed

Angels will help me run.
Run barefoot across this field.
I can hear him behind me,
He is looking for me.
My body is weak and sore,
But I keep going.
For even a mere firefly is light.
The moon is bright this evening.
I am behind her.
She is guiding me,
To the Star.
She is,
Helping me to Freedom.

Friends in Need
Connor Bryant

I am a child
Trying to save my tears
Because more pain is sure to come
Deaths and losses
of so many
of my friends
Leaving me devastated

We have but one wish,
no more bloodshed
To be free

Gets You Moving
Devi Vaddadi

War gets you moving.
There are lines…
boundaries to keep
you in line.
New lines that are
made everyday.
You must be strong to
find peace,
in a war that keeps
you moving.

Help
Kyle Potak

Help
Families fighting for their freedom
Feeling desperate and hopeless
While children are filled with fear
Frightened and without hope
You hear the cry from the deaths of friends
Disbelief that they are gone
Fighting for freedom
Help stop the devastation
Help

Help Me
Cora Christian

The tears hit me softly
The journey has just begun
The question between life or death
Help me Lord
I need you now
More than ever

Help Wanted
Kira Warner

Help is needed everywhere.
Across the world for each boy and girl.
Right now Darfur needs our support
Adults and children everywhere,
are frightened, scared, and in danger.
They need a friend.
Someone who won't scream,
but someone who will take a stand
and unite with them.
Please help the people of Darfur and
save them from this dangerous war

Home
Georgia Underhill

Why isn't it coming true?
Home turns upon me
My life feels turned around
Where am I?
Why is it so different?
Old memories are now fairytales
The castle falls to the ground
The King and Queen have left in shame
I suffer loss and hardship
and wonder…
Where is my fairytale?

Hope
Emily Galzerano

Imagine.
A bear without its claws,
no point to its life.
A bird without its wings,
feeling worthless.
Imagine.
Yet the children suffering still have hope.
I'm a child.
A child with a strong voice
and a message of hope.
A world with a path to follow.
A path of hope.
The world today needs a hero.

Hope and Courage
Natalie Kim

You must feel empty inside.
Somebody
has taken your home,
your belongings,
and your freedom.
But, there is one thing
that is very special
that can't ever be
taken from you.
That is your
hope and courage.
For as many things
that they take from you...
hope and courage
are the most precious items
you could ever have.
If you
believe and trust
in that long enough...
you will have your freedom.

Hope Is In The Air
Carey Meyers

Death is everywhere
It's in the ground
And in the air
But somehow hope still covers
this deathly air
For hope is everywhere
It's in the ground and in the air
Yet it's also in the one place death
is not
In the spirit of everyone
everywhere
Freedom is my hope
The freedom I will go home to my
bed
And the freedom to go anywhere I
please
Should a child go through this?

Hope Is Light
Surya Gourneni

Hope is a light
Its illumination can change the world
It must stay bright to guide
The way to peace
The glow will brighten the world
Hope is the light

I Am
Hannah Hart

Sitting on the grass
The game is over
I am tired
Tired of running
I need to rest
Tired of not sleeping
I am thirsty
Tired of not drinking
The game is over

I Must Be Brave
Sara Connors

My mother has told me
that the death of many people
is near.
I start to cry again.
I tell myself,
I have to stop crying,
I must be brave.
I must be brave for me,
my family,
and for the people
of my country.

I Walk Alone
Madison Smith

The path I am taking
is lonely.
It takes patience and hope,
to make the journey.

I walk…
wondering what will happen.
I hope to find peace.
A pathway to freedom.

I Would
Sumaat Khan

If I were your tear that drops to the floor,
I would wash away your pain.
If I were your imagination,
I would soar to a peaceful place.
If I were your voice,
I would shout to the world.
If I were your eyes,
I would see only love.
If I were your spirit,
I would be a light.

Ice
Dennis Chan

The game has started.
The referee is not paying attention.
The opposing team hits the puck
before we check.
The puck slides across the ice
The other team scores.
My team is playing fair
We know we have the spirit to win.
We need the referee to open his eyes.
We know we have the courage to win.

I'm Coming Home
Tierney Alexis Thompson

My body can't take it
Tears are falling
Blood is pouring
I'm coming home

I am no longer afraid
I am ready to see my family
Peace is near
I'm coming home

In Need of a Hero
Sabrina Duff

One day I woke up in my mother's arms.
We were being taken away from my home.
Help!
We need a hero.
All I want is to be home and free.
Tears are dripping down my face.
Help, we need a hero.
I think of the freedom.
I have faith that the world
will send a hero.
It is hard to be patient,
but I believe you
will send a hero.
We need a hero.

In the Distance
Amulya Yalamanchili

In the distance he awaits.
Dark, cloudy, and blurry.
By dawn, his soul will be gone.
His spirit will fly throughout the night.
Windy and cold.
Friends and family
kneel at his grave.
Tears in their eyes.
Lonely.

In the World
Erik Thysse

Love
Love is the will in all living things
Heroes thrive on love
Without love
In the world
There can be no peace

Journey to Hope
Emily O'Brien

The journey to hope is frightening,
a search for a place of freedom
The path is dark with many curves,
it is like trying to run on quicksand
Shadows fill the darkness,
coming to snatch all hope.
Heroes are like the morning,
they are coming.

Journey To Peace
Travis Wright

The journey to world peace
may be long.
The path can be grueling and
the destination can seem very far away.
But… you must keep traveling
on your journey to peace.

Just Emptiness
Neha Agrawal

The spider webs have fallen.
The breeze is just a chill.
The petals turned to dust.
The rain has stopped.
The village is in ruins.
There is just emptiness.

Knocking
John Craytor

Tears fall
As the sadness knocks on the doors
of the Sudanese
We must unite
and save a nation
Persistence is all we need
Save the Sudanese
Because if just one of us is not free
None of us are

Let Peace Fall
Hannah Vargas

You see the light of a firefly.
The moon with such darkness.
Eyes filling with tears.
Children's faces full with tears.
The loss of a life,
a child.
Let peace fall
For now there are empty lives.

Life of A Child
Michelle Kwak

A life of a child
careless and free
not watchful and restricted
filled with adventure and discovery
not of concern and sadness
filled with brightness
not darkness
The life of a child

Live to Die
Mark Bourdelais

I hear guns outside.
I run to the window.
I see people running.
I run with them.
I need agility and courage.
Will I make it?

Losing Game
William Harris

In a game of chess,
players are playing to win.
The board is set.
I look down and see that my
knights, bishops, and queen
have disappeared.
All I have is my king and pawns.
The fight is difficult and hopeless.
Soon, my opponent takes them away.
Leaving me
to lose the game.
The game of life…

Lost Somewhere
Rebecca Park

I'm lost somewhere
I can't find my way
I hope someone is praying for me
As I would do for them
I just hope
I'll be free someday
I ran away from my burning house
I ran with a tear-stained face
Hoping to see my way
I'm lost somewhere

Lost Soul
Jimmy Hennessey

My life is empty
It left with the mist
at dawn
With my soul

Missing
Colm Gallagher

The night is empty, not a sound.
There is no one but my mom and me.
My dad is lost, he must be found.
At the break of dawn his body is on the ground.
His body is empty but his soul is full.

Moonlit Night
Megan McDevitt

A waterfall of
children's tears.
For they have nothing.
The moon
shines brightly over
this land.
A light of hope.
Hope,
for the people.
Soon... the door of opportunity
will open and
people will be free.

My Courage
Priya Chandrashekar

My courage is building up
It is like a bird that has learned how to fly
I hope my journey will be safe.
I have dreamed of this day,
The day to escape
Finally, the bird soars alone.
I thought at night as I gazed at the stars
I imagined how it would be to be free,
Now it is time to be free.

My Grandpa's Soul
Elijah Gadsden

My grandpa died fighting for my life.
Clear tears slide down my face.
I see his soul outside in the field.
He is in a better place.
I'm lucky, knowing he will
always be here for me.

My Greatest Fear
Nigel Velasquez

When it is night imagine a fight
Soldiers tell others that they need courage.
I see their tears
They fear that they will lose.

Some say, I am brave…
They give prayers to God.
When I look at myself I say, "I need hope".
I think of a silver path of sadness
And I cry from the despair.

My Hope
Omar Abdelfattah

I don't have the energy
or my freedom.
Somebody took it away.
I hope someone will help me.
I can't save myself.
I don't have the energy
My only hope is that
it's not too late to become a hero.

My Sad Life; Away From Home
Crawford Sonderegger

I am on a path,
The path of light,
The violence I must face,
I am walking away,
From their dark hearts,
I have just one wish,
" *Become a friend, enemies,*
Become a friend..."
I'm still searching,
For freedom,
On this path,
Where there is
Loss...
But one day,
A group of heroes,
Will come to save,
me... and my family.

Myself
Sonya Ali

I see myself in the stars.
I am clear of thoughts,
in a trance.
My mind wishes
that it was in control.
Now, I think of the many choices
I have made,
as I walk down the path.

31

Oh, Love
Colin Schmetzer

Oh, love
Oh, love
please come and rescue me.
I trust you to come
and give me freedom
With your
brave heart you will rescue me.
Please walk with me
on the
trail of freedom.

One By One
Elizabeth Reid

Have faith in yourself.
Even though
you may have fear.
Your hope will help you.
It will guide you
like the North Star.
Have courage, be strong.
When you number the stars,
one by one.

One Violent Night
Emily Jimenez

One violent night
I lay in my bed
in the stillness of the darkness
Suddenly, dad raced into my room
with a vision of fear in his eyes.
We started our journey
to a safer place.
I didn't know where.
I had to be brave.
We had to trust each other
and no one else.
With tears in our eyes, safe at last.
Wondering when and if we can go home.
Because home should mean
we are safe.

Open Field
Michael Holohan

Here I am
On the open field
There is only stillness
I'm nervous
Why is the crowd staring at
me?
Stillness
My friends, Where are they?
Stillness
 I just want to play.
Why isn't anyone here?
Stillness
I yell and nobody hears me.
My childhood must be over
What happened?
Stillness

Out Of Control
Jordyn Gates

Darfur is spinning
out of control.
Why do we
refuse to look?
The government is not
playing by any rules.
The world is spinning
out of control.

Peace
Brandon Kelly

Not everything is clear.
I have to accept the truth.
But I wish the earth
was united.
If people tried
there could be peace.
The world is a beautiful place
if people would cooperate.
There is so much rage.
May the anger disappear.

Peace in the World
Fayzan Sabri

The love in our world has been lost,
For such violence shall not continue like this,
Would anyone welcome such violence and fighting
in their own homes?
Families will be horrified
Tears and crying shall be heard,
Even your own family will be touched.

Power
Heather Cockrell

If I had the power
I would create a path home for you
The path of love
The path of peace
The path that unites the world
One path

Protected By An Angel
Todd Craig

I am protected
Protected by an angel
The love of angels
will carry me to safety
Their wings are whiter than snow
They lift me up from my sorrows
They are there to guide me to peace

Racing Fear
Robert Owens

heart, beating fast
fear, racing
pounding with worry
skin, dirty
covered in stench
dripping with sorrow
eyes, burning
filled with rage
foggy with sadness

Red Flames
Kate Rasmussen

In my dreams I see red flames from my past
This fire has scorched my life
It appears and I cannot forget the intensity
My heart feels like it is lost in the blaze
Searching for a home
A home without an inferno

Sadness
Skanda Setty

I see sadness
People that are without a home
Nothing seems to change
At sunrise they are still homeless.
The light seems dark
I see no hope

Sailing Love
Isabella Testere

Love sails on
through the pain.
Like a boat on a river
where there are two paths.
You could take
the bumpy, wavy one
or the smooth and calm one.
The path you choose can be
the one of love and hope.

Shadows of the Night
David Caldwell

Everything is still.
Shadows of the night
do not move.
We fear that they may find us
on our long journey.
They're out there somewhere,
but where?
Shadows of the night.

Spirit
Mitchell Diep

Is your spirit
still inside of you?

I will be the traveler
to help you find it.
Walk down the path and
you will see me there.

On this path
I will bring dreams
that you thought you lost.
Your spirit is inside you.

Spirit Chaser
Eric Crisp

I am chasing a spirit
It has stolen my soul
My soul
It flies
Weaving back and forth between the stars
It is too fast
Tears cool and crisp roll down my cheeks
I hear a cry
Good spirits
They get my soul back
My tears are gone
No spirits
Just me and the stars

Spirit of a Hero
Daniel Tan

Brave and still.
You hear a horrifying cry,
a signal that violence awaits you.
Unseen army?
It comes from the darkness,
a death has occurred.
Frightened by the voice,
the path awaits you.
A grave appears,
but the spirit of a hero is still there.

Spring Dreams
Nick Mutton

As I walked barefoot
the words
came to me
Dreams
The sunrise was beautiful
The grass was green
The mist was in my soul
And in the distance I could hear
Spring.
Then I see a star
It is like a dream
Growing and collecting dreams
Until the end
The end
when everything stops
And dreams happen

Stillness
K.J. Rau

In the very stillness of the night,
It is the calmness that scared me.
"I must be brave," I tell myself.
The tears run down my cheeks
as fast as I run away from them.
I saw the shadowy outline of a body.
They are here!
I hear screams
Fear and sadness
soaking up the hours of darkness.
Stillness returns to the night.

Stolen
Chris Wiger

There have been
many deaths and
most are unseen.
This world is ignoring their
voices.
Their entire lives have
been stolen.

Stormy Life
Natalie Salter

I know your family is crying
Pounding tears
Stormy Life
Puzzling
This violent storm has brought you
The winds of change
The hammering rain has flooded your life
The thunder crackles above you
Like the sound of war
The bright lightning flashes through the sky
Reminding you that there is no peace

Sunrise
Malik Piersol

The beautiful mist
of the African morning.
The wind on my face reminds me
there is an angel.
The sunrise brings me courage for the day.
The tree branches unite,
giving me peace.
The sky darkens and the stars glow side by side,
reminding me of my hopes and dreams.

Support
Joey Pappagallo

They travel a great distance
to find freedom.
Instead, they find dryness
Little to eat
Nothing to drink
Like a ship that has wrecked
No hope
No support
Nobody is there for them
They are helpless.

Tears
Mandy Wright

In the moonlight,
You can see a firefly.
But in Darfur,
Only you remain in the dark.
Can you see the children's tears?
They are unhappy.
Can you see it?
Everyone else can.

The Beginning
Lucas Martin

There is death all around
Tears of pain
Flood the camps
Anger is filling the war
Peace is slow in arriving.

The Distance
Jake Wille

We must choose a path.
There is no time to wait.
We must take a journey.
The violence is growing.
We hear a cry in the distance.
There is just more death.
We must respond.

The Empty Bowl
Sam Allen

Family, I have no more
All died in pain and grief.
Starving, Dying, Starving.
Thick tears
roll down my face
My life is shadowed
The fighting
The death,
All memories now.
I fled from home
I ran away
And now I wonder
Should I have stayed
and died?
My life is shadowed
Covered up.
An empty bowl
Where there was fruit
There's only darkness.
Empty Bowl.

The Game
Ani Surumpudi

The opponents are moving towards the goal.
The score… nobody cares.
They always cheat.
They push, trip, and tackle.
The referee… gives no red card.
Without warning
the opponent takes the home team away….
never to be seen again.

The Gift
Abi Hamal

We will help you regain your freedom.
Maybe you will help us one day,
as we did for you.
Freedom rings in our country,
we will help it ring in yours.
To be free is a gift,
We will give you that gift.

The Girl in the Distance
Sydney Smedley

I see a girl in the distance.
She is screaming.
I don't know why.

I don't know who she is,
but she does remind me
of somebody.

Now she's gone into
the darkness of
the night's mist.

 Now I know who
she reminds me of…
myself.

The Hardships of the Dawn of Life
Sarah Doyon

Deep within
many souls
is a misty hardship,
that the Dawn of Life brings.
Peace, Courage, and Hope will come
if we realize that sometimes
the world is wrong.
They'll come
but we must try very hard.
For Peace, Courage, and Hope don't come
at one's request of righteousness

The Moon
Jesika DeDonato

I look through my telescope
The lenses are making it blurry
But, as it becomes clearer
I see the stars missing from the sky
Then, the lenses go blurry again
It wants me not to see
I continue to look and search for the moon
With stars missing from the sky

The Movie
Janelle Batz

The movie started five years ago.
Won't it ever stop?

Why is the popcorn sold out?
Why is the candy left on a shelf?
Where is the audience?
Doesn't anyone care?

The movie just keeps playing
over and over.
Won't it ever stop?

45

The Passage to Freedom
Laura Pax

Grasp tightly to hope,
Make it as strong as a cheetah
Plummeting through the dark woods.

Push away fear with a confident hand,
Tell it that you are too smart to be ensnared
By its greasy fingers.

Hold fast to your wish,
A wish for a clearer future,
Show them how brightly you shine,
Brighter than the shimmering night sky.

Though your tears may fall,
Let your voice be heard.
Let everyone know that you will overcome your
oppressors,
And live again in a land more abundant
Than the Garden of Perfection.

The Starving Village
Juan Ojeda

I need energy
I am starving and there
is nothing to eat
I need energy
to walk
but I have none.
It feels like I
have died
and I am in my grave.
But I am
brave and I will
find more energy

The Truth
Kyle Albers

In this life of violence and death
my family is now nothing
but a dream.
There's no one to talk to
but my shadow.
I'm frightened and scared.
My bravery diminishes
with every tear I shed.
This is the truth
of my life.

The Violence is Ending
Marcel Steele

The distance is great,
but be patient.
A hero,
strong with force
can support your invisible, frightened spirit.
You can be free,
the violence is ending,
peace is coming.
Don't cry,
the bloodshed is ending
in your persistent,
horrifying world.

The Wall
Victor Wang

The journey lies ahead.
The stars are bright,
just like your dreams.
There is a wall
between love and hate.
The world is still choosing one side.
The sky is clear,
just like your hopes.
The spirits of Darfur
shall never be lost.

The War
Chase Davidson

Graves are everywhere.
I am trapped and feel helpless.
I have been waiting for peace
for such a long time.
Now shadows of my family
surround me.

The Weight of the World

Matt Dapper
Nicole Levinrad
Jake Lewis
Kaylyn Thomas

At night they are
on the run.
Safety is their goal.
The weight of the world
is on their shoulders.
They only hope
that in the end,
there will be light.
They only hope to find peace.

The Wish

Emily Rivera

How I wish I didn't see
the image of the girl in the shadow.
She had fear in her eyes and had stillness,
like when you find out
what death is like.
How I wish she were alive.

The Woods
Shelby Thompson

Once upon a time,
there was a princess.
Her mother died, and her life changed.
Because of jealousy, her life was in danger.
She fled to the woods out of fear for her life.
She lives day to day.
She always worries.
She feels fear.
She misses her family.
She is always hungry.
She is scared of the new queen…
Can she ever return to her castle?

The World
Joyce Behrens

The world should be full of peace,
instead of wars and battles.
Everyone should have freedom,
instead of being held hostage.
Without violence in the world,
the tears will stop flowing.

Through My Heart
Kai Fletcher

I can hear your sadness
Through my heart
And your family and friends' too
I see your bravery
Through my heart
I can envision your freedom
Through my heart
Soon you will have your freedom

Trusting
Brennan Maxwell

In the mist
I lay in my grave
Still as a stone
But my soul is alive
Floating in the sky
Looking for hope
Trusting that it will be found

Truth
Kayleigh Pridemore

I love having the thought of him
in my mind all the time.
I see his spirit rise
All the energy he put into this Earth
is still not lost.
I know the truth even though
it is not told.
I know I will see him again
Even if I don't know when.
All I will remember
are the smiles and the laughter,
and that
is the truth.

Unseen
Isabella Young

He is unseen
But always there,
He takes care of me
So very well,
He sends heroes to fight
For our rights,
He sees children
Crying in the night,
He washes tears from our face,
He gave us
The gift of prayer,
He is unseen.

Voice of Peace
Mike Nadim

You are not alone
Your dreams are with you
They are not lost
I am your friend and
I will not be silent
I will be your voice
The voice of peace

War
Paulina Le

There's hope
And there's peace
But in war
No one is free
Be brave
It's okay
Love

Love is what I
want the world to be
Children will
Live in peace
Oh I wish,
Wish the world
Was full
Of love

War in Darfur
Megan Gossfeld

It simply cannot be true
That it's okay to hurt others
How'd you like it if it were you?

To have a united world
We need peace and harmony
How can anyone kill another person?

I think we should help
I swear an oath to stop this
I'll try my best, won't you?

We Will Continue
Christina M. Tharp

I lie awake sometimes at night,
dreaming of peace
that some do not have.
Without the peace
their lives are but nightmares,
screaming for safety, love and no more tears.
In a world full of pain and suffering,
they dream of peace, that someday will come.
Our hearts go out and our prayers
will continue, for the children of Darfur.

When?
Vamsi Veeramasu

Violence is everywhere around me.
I am longing for peace.
I know that all wars end.
But, how much blood
will sink into the earth
before there is peace?

Where Are You?
Bryan Magnuson

Nobody can hear my cry.
I am suffering in a
field of death.
I am standing in a
barren meadow.
Trees of fire
burn my life.
A river of sadness
fills with tears.
Where are you?

54

Where is the Love?
Kaynad Ahmed

We're in a world
of fear and war
Where crying and hatred
surround us.
The only thing people
are praying for
is their own safety.
Where is the love?

Wish
Scott Harrison Seigel

Wish for anything...
To have a voice for the world to hear?
The solution is not war
Violence is a light bulb that we wish
would never glow
Unite, we all must
Wish for anything...

Wonderful World
Harpreet Singh

A wonderful world
Would have peace and tranquility
Enough for everyone
All would be happy
People would start to pay forward
A wonderful world
Everyone would have kind hearts
And helping hands
People would never hurt each other
A wonderful world

Wondering When
Kaylan Manley

Here we go again,
another death has happened.
I am horrified.
But... I feel fortunate
that I still have my family.
My heart feels empty
Why shouldn't it?
I've lost almost everything
I am filled with fear
Wondering when will it end?

Words Instead of Violence
Brandon Duong

Africans are fleeing their homes,
going to bed hungry and thirsty,
getting sick and dying.
All of them are thinking one thing,
"This is the worst thing that's ever happened to me."
We must help instead of harm.
Instead of fighting
we should be talking.
We are people.
All of us are killing each other
and for what?
Land, religion, and freedom.
You can share land,
 believe in what you want
and peacefully protest for freedom.
We should help those who need help
and start arguing with words instead of violence.
Let them return to their homes
Do something!
But the question is...will you?

World of Darkness
Alexandra Nguyen

A world of darkness
Is a world of pain
Waiting for something
But the world is not yet giving
Hold on tight
Do not let it go
On your long journey
Hope is waiting for you

Written Everywhere
Faiza Khanim

I could see the stars, from my bed.
Then the sky turned to darkness.
I saw a traveler, up in the sky.
She saw all these choices to pick from.
Even I saw all the choices.
They were written,
written everywhere.
They were following her,
but the path taken was
not her choice.

Your Star
Michael Martinez

Your heart is your star,
Where your thoughts get their hope.
Dreams revolve around it and are drawn to it.
Fear is nothing... hope triumphs.
Courage is the attitude,
a sense of pride for your dreams.
Love leads you away from darkness.
Belief is what gives you your star's light.
Dreams revolve around it.

Acknowledgments

As teachers you hope that the students in your class walk away with more than learning the difference between an adverb and adjective. We hoped that this project would teach the students to use their voices to benefit others. It never dawned on us that the students would be the ones who taught us. They taught us how to be courageous and always have hope.

This book is a culmination of the effort, love, and support of many people. Thank you to everyone who touched and inspired this project.

Paul Vickers, Greg West, and Garett Brazina- for believing in this book and trusting your teachers to present such a difficult topic.

Mill Run Faculty, Parents, and Community- for every gesture and kind word.

Aisha Bain, Jen Marlowe, and Adam Shapiro- this book would have never happened had it not been for your documentary and book. Your courage and determination to share your experience in Darfur inspired us all. Thank you for being such big supporters of this book.

Dr. Maya Angelou- for a lifetime of using your words to inspire and change lives.

Dr. Donald Gallehr, Mark Farrington, and the Northern Virginia Writing Project- for encouraging teachers to take risks with writing in their classrooms.

Lois Lowry- for writing such a powerful book about friendship and bravery.

Congressman Frank Wolf and Dan Scandling- for embarking on your journey to Darfur and sharing your stories with us.

Albert &Velma Nellum, Diane & Richard Rovang, and Nancy Williams- for teaching us how to take risks. Your lives have inspired us.

Bob Cohencious and everyone at CPTV- for helping us to spread this message.

Tri-State Litho and Kumar Persad- for working so diligently to expedite the printing of this project. We are truly grateful.

Loudoun County Public Library- for encouraging us to share this book.

Loudoun County Public Schools- for supporting this project and creating a wonderful learning environment for students and teachers.

Bettie Stegall and Milde Waterfall- for being amazing teachers and bringing our poetry into your classrooms.

Thomas Jefferson School of Science and Technology Students- thank you for taking the time to critique all the poems. We could have never completed this project without all of the following students: Spencer Adams, Mike Bazarov, Zachary Batts, Matthew Bikoff, Eleanor Blakeslee, Nancy Blanford, John Bui, Matthew Chamberlain, Sylvia Chen, Samuel Clamons, Blaire Claytor, Lucas Carreno, Ronnie Cohen, Karri DeSelm, Katherine Dove, David English, Konrad Ess, Justin Etkin, Claire Eudy, Jennifer Fang, Emilia Gillevet, Wade Gong, Jessica Gorman, Paul Grimm, Craig Haseler, Zoe Hoffman, Katherine Hsu, Paul Im, Emily Jacobson, Rebecca Justin, Jane Kim, Yoosin Kim, David Klayton, Peter Kole, Jordan Kramer, Brian Lee, LeeAnn Li, Xiao Lin, Mary Linnell, Jacob McAuliffe, Katherine McLaughlin, Vanessa Miller, Stephanie Nguyen, Crystal Noel, Aditya Palepu, Molly Patterson, Brian Peppiatt, Alissa Perman, Gregory Romais, Alexandria Ruth, Lauren Ruth, Min Hyuk Seo, Mel

Sparrow, Arjun Sreekumar, Irene Tai, Narendra
Tallapragada, Anthony Tran, Stephanie Valarezo, Gregory
Vernon, Natalie Villacorta, Mariah Walker, John Walsh,
Maya Wei, Rodney Williams, Alexander Witko, Lauren
Wolbarsht, So-Jung Youn, and Harry Zhang.

We also express our gratitude to:
Catherine Adams, Jeff Aebi, Wyndi Anderson, David
Arbogast, Soren Bakken, Tri Bostelman, Janet Braverman,
Suzie Brick, Felicia Brower, Bettie Burditte, Wayde Byard,
Mary Ann Cannon, Charlie Calton, Patricia Casey, CiCi's
Pizza- Cumberland, Maryland, Ronnie Jacobs Cohen,
Holly Colbert, John Cornely, Jim Cornish, D-Hall All-
Stars, Laura Damewood, Roger Drew, Julie Edstrom,
Tammy Fossett, Brian Germain, Heather Hapworth,
Mickey Held, Catherine Holohan, Linda Holtslander,
Carol-Anne Kaye, Deneen Kellen, Megan Kuhn, Kerry
Lennon, Kim McDevitt, Maria McVicker-Roberts, Jessica
Mohr, Adam Nashban, Kristen Neely, Michelle Nyhuis,
Becky Page, Susan Panetti, Brian Peppiatt, Carolyn Perry,
Rachel Piro, Carolyn Podgorsky, Denise Pappagallo, SSN
Consulting, Julia Rastelli, Mark Rogers, Pamela Rogg,
Jackie Schmetzer, Elise Schroeder, Arthur Scott, Sarah
Simmons, Todd Snead, Sharon Sovereign, Kadie Summers-
Jones, Sunlight Nail Supply, Rhonda Thomason, United
States Holocaust Memorial Museum, Laura Warner,
Melissa West, Nancy Wikle, and Jim Wolslayer.

-L.W., R.W., A.W.